Hear The Father

Rise Beyond Self

ISBN: 979-8-9989067-1-8

Dedication

Hear The Father, Rise Beyond Self, is dedicated to Barbara Johnson Burnette and Lori Webster, who were born to be my sisters, and Claudette Edwards, who was born to become my sister. You are three amazing women, who each in her own unique and special way kept me grounded in who I am to understand and come to know whose I am.

I love you all and will forever be grateful to God for knitting us together.

Set your mind on things above, not on things on the earth
Colossians 3:2 (NKJV)

Life Through Song
"Testify to Love" - Wynonna Judd

FOREWORD

When Jana first shared her vision for *Hear The Father, Rise Beyond Self* with me, I was immediately struck by her passion, clarity and deep reverence for God's word. Having known her for over thirty years, I've witnessed firsthand her unwavering commitment to understanding the relationship our Heavenly Father desires with His children.

One thing that has always stood out about Jana is her persistence in seeking divine understanding. She would remain immersed in a topic, pondering Scripture and conversing with the Lord, until the day came when she would joyfully declare, "I got it! I know what the Lord is saying," or, "I finally understand what the Bible means by this." Jana never speaks or teaches on something until she has fully grasped its meaning—an extraordinary quality that reflects both her humility and devotion. That is the kind of woman she is. That is my friend, Jana L. Johnson.

Hear The Father, Rise Beyond Self, is a reflection of her heart, wisdom and a lifelong journey of walking with God. Through its pages, she takes you on a powerful journey through her life, navigating roads paved with music and songs that have not only inspired her but also deepened her relationship with God. You will see how each song became a stepping stone, revealing profound spiritual truths and illuminating her path to greater understanding.

More than just a testimony, *Hear The Father, Rise Beyond Self,* is an invitation. It will encourage you to persevere through any obstacle that tries to hinder your destiny in Christ. Jana's passion for connecting people with both the Old and New Testaments shines through every chapter, setting readers on a pathway to true discipleship. *Hear The Father, Rise Beyond Self*, is filled with love, hope, and faith—woven together as a testament to God's faithfulness.

I still remember the first time I met Jana—her passion for life was contagious, filling the room with energy and purpose. Today, she shares that same passion with everyone who picks up *Hear The Father, Rise Beyond Self*. As you turn these pages, prepare to be drawn closer to God, to deepen your understanding of what it truly means to be not just saved, but a devoted Disciple of Jesus Christ.

I am honored to introduce you to this incredible work. May it bless, challenge, and inspire you as much as it has inspired me.

Min. Lennon E. McDuffie

PROLOGUE

"Look What You've Done" - Tasha Layton

God's Story
"Papa Can You Hear Me" - Barbra Streisand

In 2020, I wrote *I Heard You, Daddy: Lessons Learned From My Grandfather*, my story of how I came to know God's Word. Even though that was my second book, I still never really thought of myself as a writer. So, when God told me there was another book in me, I was not happy. For two years, He handed me fragments that did not seem to fit together. I knew He said to begin on September 16, 2024, yet for weeks I wrestled with what to say, how to say it, and why it had to be me.

Then, at 1:00 am on September 16, I woke with a heavy heart. The weight had started the morning before while watching an Atlanta Sunday program. A well-known woman shared that colleagues had called her too passionate and too expressive. Only after seeing another woman lead with that same fire did she feel she had permission to be her authentic self.

My heart ached. I asked God, why would anyone need permission to be who they are. His answer was simple: This is why you will write, and this is how you will begin.

People who love me are sometimes amused, sometimes horrified, that I will talk to anyone, anywhere. My hope is that this book speaks to you the way God speaks to me. That you will know you do not need anyone's permission to be authentically you. What is for you is for you, and only you can live your destiny.

The first time God whispered the seed of this book; I had just finished a weekend of deep cleaning. I thought, so this is how Cinderella must have felt. A little while later, I heard, "God's Cinderella." I did not yet know what that meant, or that the image would become a way to explain how God's purpose finds us.

Cinderella began as a beloved daughter, living a happy life with her father. After he died, her world turned upside down. She went from lady of the manor to servant by the hearth, named Cinderella for the cinders that kept her warm. She had every reason to become bitter. She did not. She gave away what little she had and kept her heart soft. Even in her worst season, she chose joy, and she believed that change would come.

Imagine that was you. In your most difficult season, who do you become? The life you are living may not be the life you expected. How you respond will shape where you are able to go. Just like Cinderella, you must find joy in your circumstances. "Rejoice always, pray without ceasing, in everything give thanks; for this is the will of God in Christ Jesus for you." (Thessalonians 5:16–18, NKJV)

Your life is not about the version you are trying to hold together of yourself. It is about who God created you to be and the purpose attached to your name.

Everything Cinderella needed was already in her. Everything we need has already been placed in us. God is and always will be with us. When we feel lost or overwhelmed, we can dig deep and remember we are not alone.

Nothing catches God by surprise. There is purpose in all things, and He will use every snippet in its time. "Rest in the Lord, and wait patiently for Him, do not fret because of him who prospers in his way, because of the man who brings wicked schemes to pass. (Psalm 37:7, NKJV)

Trouble begins when we try to bend circumstances to our will. For a while, things may look as we hoped, but that moment always ends. If we refuse to learn what God is teaching, we circle back to the same place until His purpose in that season is complete. We can stack up accomplishments and still miss what was meant only for us if we do it in a way God did not intend. The world offers what we think we want. God gives what He knows we need—aplenty.

What if Cinderella had grown hard and unkind? The friends who would one day help her transform were part of her story from the beginning. Would they have shown up if she had let the cruelty of others reshape her? Only God knows the hour when our change will come.

In every moment, we can ask: Am I doing this as God intends? "For the vision is yet for an appointed time; but at the end it will speak, and it will not lie, though it tarries, wait for it; because it will surely come, it will not tarry." (Habakkuk 2:3, NKJV)

From beginning to end, God shows us how to do it His way through His word. Waiting is not easy. Yes, you can make something happen faster, but it will not be what it should be or could have been. After years of struggle and waiting, Cinderella received abundance. She felt her pain and still found joy. She trusted that change would come. At the right time, you will receive what was established only for you.

Do you want the checkbox of achievements, or the blessings that come from waiting with God? Let your tears cleanse your soul as you wait for His perfect time. Your story is still unfolding. In His time, you can have more than just good enough.

ACT I

AWARENESS

"Then the eyes of those who see will no longer be closed, and the ears of those who hear will listen."

(Isaiah 32:3 NIV)

Chapter 1

Foundations of Love in Silence

"God is in This Story" - Katy Nichole & Big Daddy Weave

From the time I was a child, silence became my sanctuary. I could sit in a room filled with people for hours without uttering a word, content to observe. Even now, I can lose myself in the quiet act of listening. I have come to believe this was God's way of training me, showing me that if I slowed down long enough, I could see the true heart of people.

I grew up in the warmth and chaos of a large extended family. My mother, my two sisters, my grandparents, aunts, uncles, cousins, and my great aunt and great uncle all played a part in shaping who I would become. Ours was not a family that said "I love you" often, but love pulsed beneath every interaction. Alive in acts of sacrifice, in meals shared around the table, in the insistence that we look out for one another.

My grandfather was consistent and uncompromising, while my grandmother was his gentler half, patient and kind. They were never divided, never swayed by outside voices. My great aunt and great uncle mirrored that loyalty in quieter ways. Together, those four, along with my mother, became the bedrock of my life.

Each of them taught me something essential. My grandfather instilled integrity and the courage to be true to myself. My grandmother modeled goodness. My great aunt embodied generosity. My great uncle revealed quiet strength. My mother was my fiercest protector. Through her, I learned resilience, advocacy and the kind of forgiveness that refuses to grow bitter.

In such a big family, individuality was hard to come by. My sisters and I were often lumped together as one, "BarbaraJanaLori," as if our names were a single word. I longed for room to be my own person. I understood who I was inside, but did not know how to express it in ways others could hear. So, I turned inward. I let silence speak for me. It was protection. It was where God began whispering truths I would not fully recognize until much later.

What others did not see was that silence was not emptiness. The silence made them sad and upset them, yet they did not use the silence to help them understand. I know what they thought: heartless, emotionless, "that's just Jana" is what they would say. How could they understand what I could not explain? All that time listening, watching, was God showing me how to shield my heart.

The heart is our life's blood. God is love, love that keeps our blood flowing and our hearts strong. God's home for His Spirit. The heart is our most fragile possession and yet one we are the most careless of protecting.

We know things about life and people deep in our hearts. We ignore that knowledge because it does not take us in the direction, we think we should go. Instead of being guided by what we know in our heart, we guide our heart to feel what we want to believe.

Emotions can make us feel wonderful, then use those same feelings to destroy us. "Keep your heart with all diligence, for out of it spring the issues of life." (Proverbs 4:23)

Strength of heart is not being led by fleeting emotions. We have to reposition God from our head into our heart. "My flesh and my heart fail; but God is the strength of my heart and my portion forever." (Psalm 73:26 NKJV)

Yes, God knows your heart. The question now becomes, does God have your heart?

Chapter 2

The Call in Childhood

"Greatest Love of All" - George Benson

I always thought I was two years old when my parents separated. In my fifties, during a conversation with my aunt, I learned I was two months old, and my father tried to keep me. Now in my sixties, God shows me that was the first time He brought me out of Egypt. Of course, being two months old, I was unaware of everything.

From my very beginning, God has been trying to keep me as His own, keep me on my path of purpose. At two months old, God took me from the man He chose to birth me and placed me in the midst of the man He chose to give me life. My earliest memories of faith are simple. My grandfather prayed over meals, and a Bible was kept on his nightstand with whispered prayers before bed. Church visits were occasional and maybe on special occasions.

At eight years old, my mother sent me to Vacation Bible School. I may not have seemed attentive, but I was paying attention. When the teacher told me I had learned nothing, she was wrong. The Word had entered. It simply had not yet taken root.

God called me again during that time, when He showed me the disastrous outcome of drug use. At twelve, I went to see *The Wiz* with Stephanie Mills. When she sang "Home," something deep inside me stirred. I did not have words for it, but now I know it was God.

At sixteen, standing in the mirror, combing my hair, I listened to George Benson's "The Greatest Love of All." As the lyrics washed over me, I realized I could love myself as I was. A truth my grandfather had spoken for years. I thought a song had given me courage. I know now it was God calling, trying to anchor me before the enemy snatched me away. "He who is of God hears God's words; therefore, you do not hear, because you are not of God." (John 8:47 NKJV)

At each of these moments, God had His eye on me. Even when I did not know Him for myself, He knew me. He was already writing a story I was yet to see, a story of pursuit, grace, and relentless love.

We do not know, nor can we predict the journey to our final destination. Our life here on earth is made up of never-ending twists, turns, scrapes, bruises, ups, downs and whatever else comes in between. All we can do as we take each step is be grateful for the highs and pick ourselves up from the lows.

Whatever point in time we may be, God is with us. His Spirit guides us, and Jesus waits for us with open arms. In the last line of the poem "Footprints in the Sand," "The Lord replied, 'The times when you have seen only one set of footprints, my child, is when I carried you.'" (Author Unknown) This is another example that God is always with me, a favorite poem that touched me deeply, before I knew who was carrying me.

Flaws and all, we will always be His most valuable masterpiece. His precious, priceless, greatest love.

Chapter 3

Breaking Free and Finding Self

"Stand" - Donnie McClurkin

By eighteen, I knew I could not keep shutting people out and still hope to be accepted for who I knew myself to be. I also knew I could not continue living only in reaction to what others expected.

My first major adult decision came after graduating from college and coming back home. I had to leave New York. Home was still a box— every corner crowded with obligations and memories. I longed to breathe. Miami called to me like a promise. Sunlight instead of darkness. Rippling waves instead of concrete. A place to reinvent myself.

My mother panicked. How could I move with no money, no family, no place to live? To ease her fears, I framed the move as going to graduate school. It was the truth, although getting a Master's Degree was not my goal. For me, the move was about independence. Having worked for an airline, I started traveling and discovered that while cultures differ, people are remarkably alike. And like gravitates to like. Connection is not about language or nationality. It is about the linking of spirits.

Miami became the soil where earlier lessons took root. In Miami, I found community and freedom. Immediate connections. Like-minded people who could see beyond the surface. Understand without words. Reach out, open up, and be enclosed within their circle. A new link to lifelong friendships. In Miami, I was able to explore all the thoughts and ideas locked inside me for years. Experiences and opportunities I would not have known existed if I had stayed in New York. Miami became the place where the root matured into me.

Two years later, I moved to Atlanta, expecting it to be temporary, not knowing it would be where the root would be planted. The home for me to flourish and grow.

Hearing a call to serve, I began volunteering in a deeper way. Supporting nonprofits, mentoring youth organizations, and working with seniors, it all felt like an extension of who I was meant to be.

For the next four years, my days moved the way I always envisioned. Friendships developed, work kept me on the move, a constant high on life. And when I missed my family, they were just a short plane ride away.

Until moving to Atlanta, I thought the Bible Belt meant where a lot of Bibles were sold. Well, I learned differently, even explored the church for a minute. After some of my earlier experiences with Christians, I was leery of going to church, but as they say, "When in Rome, do as the Romans do."

Going to church gave me the sense of being on a roller coaster. I was unsettled, not sure what direction to go, trying to keep up with the sudden, unexpected and nonsensical thoughts and actions of Christians. I used to like watching Jekyll and Hyde movies. I did not like being in one.

After two years, I still did not understand who or what a Christian was. Church was too inconsistent in what was said and not in line with what was seen. My grandfather taught me to stand up to what you say, say what you mean, mean what you say, and be willing to face the consequences. Church people did not seem to follow that rule. So, I decided it was time for me to get off the ride. "For by your words you will be acquitted, and by your words you will be condemned." (Matthew 12:37 NIV)

I have to admit, though I believed church was not for me, it did reinforce within me to always be true to who I am.

ACT II

ADMISSION

"What, then, shall we say in response to these things? If God is for us, who can be against us?"

(Roman 8:31 NIV)

Chapter 4

Loss, Grief and the Return to God

"The Truth" - Megan Woods

After you think you got it, you know you can conquer the world. Then you get shot down.

The greatest turning point of my adult life came with my mother's death. My world split in two, before and after Beverly Johnson.

For two years, I cried. When the tears slowed, I was exhausted by sorrow and began searching for a way out, a way forward. Then, after seventeen years of silent nudges, God came for me full force.

A friend would not stop urging me to go back to church. The same friend who convinced me to try church the first time. In my state of mind, with my mother's death still heavy on my heart, having God in my life was the last thing I wanted. Since it did not work for me before, I was not too keen to try again. So, this time, God was going to have to prove He was worth my time.

My time is valuable. If I were going to waste it going back to church, it would be on my terms. I laid out four conditions for God: a conversation with a Christian who was not preachy; a church close to home; a service that did not start before 10:00 am; and a pastor who spoke to the actual circumstances of my life.

To my surprise and annoyance, three conditions were met almost immediately. The first came at 3:00 am, while leaving Reggae SunSplash in Montego Bay, Jamaica, on a three hour bus ride back to our hotel. You can imagine my shock and awe when I realized the conversation was happening. The second came when I noticed a sign that said the church offered two services, one at 8:00 am and another at 10:00 am. A sign I never saw before on a church I had been driving by for years. Then the third came when a friend stopped by my house after visiting that same church as a possible school for her son. I was not amused, though slightly impressed with God.

The final condition required me to walk through the church doors. I did it for four weeks straight. The pastor kept saying accepting Christ is a leap of faith at the end of each service. I told myself that if he said it again next week, I would join the church.

I was so happy and extremely relieved to see a guest pastor the following Sunday. Then I was horrified when he, too, recited a version of "accepting Christ is a leap of faith."

As much as I did not want to, I honored my word. I joined the church. I could not believe that within thirty days, I was back in church. Within three months, I was baptized and serving God. He did His part, and I did mine. I surrendered. "For it is God who works in you to will and to act in order to fulfill his good purpose." (Philippians 2:13 NIV)

Looking back, I can see His Word planted in me long before I gave Him my yes. He sowed seeds that bloomed as arranged moments in a language I could understand. Scriptures from childhood, prayers whispered over me, and the faithfulness I had observed in my family had all prepared me.

What I had thought of as God's distance was patience. Grief had broken me open, and through the crack, His light entered. God does not waste our pain. He uses even our deepest sorrow to draw us closer. To restore our hope.

With the absence of my mother, I was finally able to feel the fullness of His presence. "Nevertheless, I tell you the truth; It is expedient for you that I go away: for if I go not away, the Comforter will not come unto you; but if I depart, I will send him unto you." (John 16:7- KJV)

I had to think about the power of those words for a few days. Finally, what made sense in my mind was painful but slightly fortifying. My mother, from my first breath until her last, had my back. My beginning of understanding was humbling.

Chapter 5

The Enemy's Grip and God's Pursuit

"Goodness of God" - Cece Winans

From sixteen to thirty-two, I thought the world was mine. Consequences were options I was willing to accept. I believed freedom meant doing whatever I wanted. However, the enemy is real. He is not a childhood monster or boogie man under the bed. His aim is to steal, kill, and destroy our relationship with God. "Be alert and of sober mind. Your enemy the devil prowls around like a roaring lion looking for someone to devour." (1 Peter 5:8 NIV)

For years, I let him consume me. Music, once God's language to my heart, faded into the background of the enemy's noise. I chased freedom and fun, forgetting to remember myself along the way.

The enemy is stationary, limited and loud. As he can only be in one place, he sends his minions to go where he cannot. The enemy is insidious. We have to be mindful about what we release into the atmosphere. What can quickly be grabbed to use against us. Used as a distraction to drown out that still, small voice.

The enemy really did not have to work hard with me. I already knew my life was good. All he had to do was keep the volume on high. Stop me from clearly hearing the call of God. "The Spirit of the Lord shall rest upon Him, the Spirit of wisdom and understanding, the Spirit of counsel and might, the Spirit of knowledge and of the fear of the Lord." (Isaiah 11:2, NKJV)

Unless we are listening intently to hear God, what may look or sound like His voice may be the enemy minions sent to deceive us. Listening to the enemy whisper, "It is all yours," allows him to take hold of what was never meant to be his. I let the enemy continuously use that sword on me.

The old saying, "the world is my oyster," reminds me of that season in my life. Shakespeare actually wrote in *The Merry Wives of Windsor*, "Why then the world's mine oyster, which I with sword will open."

Oysters are messy with a hard shell to shuck. In the end, you hope to find a pearl inside. I kept shucking what the world offered, convinced the next shell held the treasure. However, the world is not my oyster. The world belongs to God. The pearl of great price has already been given. "Watch and pray, lest you enter into temptation. The spirit indeed is willing, but the flesh is weak." (Matthew 26:41, NKJV)

The enemy kept me trapped, living in an illusion. Every time I came up empty. The pearls I thought I held dissolved in my hands.

The enemy is real, a master magician, determined to keep us out of reach of God. Misdirecting truth to twist reality. Enthralled in the enemy camp, God stayed connected, kept calling. He called when I was two months old and placed me close to my grandfather, who guided me by His direction. He called at eight, at twelve, at sixteen. He called through songs, music and other mediums of the arts. Through protection and through whispers I did not yet recognize. He called while the enemy kept trying to cover me in clouds of gray. The battle was never about who I was. It was always about *whose* I am.

God, in His mercy, never let me go. He kept gently calling me back, building blocks to understanding that all is already within me. The treasure is not in the oyster; the treasure is within you. The love of God. "And my God will meet all your needs according to the riches of his glory in Christ Jesus." (Philippians 4:19 NIV)

My fight with the enemy was real. It was unexpected. It was a lesson in the power of God. The enemy took hold of me and tried to take me out. A forceful energy in the room surrounded me, took hold of me. I was out of control. I had no control. And yet, as the war raged within me, encircling me were the prayers and words of God raining down on me.

I could do nothing as he tossed me around and shouted words from my mouth. I heard a loud "she's mine," then a soft "she was never yours." Then, in whispering silence, the battle was over, the battle won. I lay quiet in the stillness, as the tears fell. "Submit yourselves therefore to God. Resist the devil, and he will flee from you." (James 4:7 NKJV)

Freedom reigns.

We are God's children. He is always with us. His Spirit guides us. God may let us go our way. God will never let us walk alone. He follows at a distance, always within our reach, His Spirit, the whispers leading us home. "Be strong and of good courage, do not fear nor be afraid of them; for the Lord your God, He *is* the One who goes with you. He will not leave you nor forsake you." (Dt 31:6 NIV)

Chapter 6
Music as a Spiritual Language

"Where My Heart Will Take Me" - Russell Watson

You found God, you accepted God and allowed Him into your life. So, what comes next? Accepting God will be the beginning of the toughest fight of your life. Giving authority of your life over to a belief, a hope, an unknown truth. However, nothing worth having is ever easy, and I was never told life would be easy.

What we can control is which direction we take to remain who we are, who we should be, who we were birth to be. The enemy has nothing to do with how we start, but he will be right there trying to stop our relationship with God, determining what it will take to keep you from ever knowing and understanding whose you are. "So God created man in His *own* image; in the image of God He created him; male and female He created them." (Genesis 1:27 NKJV)

From the beginning, I only knew how to be Jana, and that has not changed in my sixty plus years. Although Jana may have strayed, gotten lost along the way, now she has found her way back to her true self.

We are born as gifts to our parents and the adults in our lives. As with any gift, what happens to us will be decided by how well they care for us. Gifts are given for a specific purpose or use; we can change how it is used, but we cannot change what it was designed to be. "Every good gift and perfect gift is from above, coming down from the Father of heavenly lights, who does not change like shifting shadows." (James 1:17 NIV)

But God, we get back up. Standing steady upon His firm foundation.

The people in my life with the greatest impact had an appreciation for God's gift. My mother, grandparents and great aunt and great uncle— these five people guided me, taught me, showed me and most importantly accepted me as I was and for who I am.

They were five such different people, but they were all truly loving people who showed their hearts in different ways. I believe who I am was meant to be a part of all of them. I will always be grateful, I can reflect on whose I am, because of the care they had for the gift God placed in their lives.

They all taught me something different about life, how to live life confident in who I am. Although I did not know at the time, the conversations we had solidified who I was and who I am still: a no-nonsense, take-no-prisoners, stand my ground, speak the truth, woman of God. "Train up a child in the way he should go, and when he is old, he will not depart from it." (Proverbs 22:6 NKJV)

God placed me in the center of these five people to show me who He is. A visual interpretation to understand the truth of whose I am. From watching them, I learned that it is not what you say. Your actions let others know who you really are through your character. Your actions give meaning to your words. By their actions being consistent with their words, I was able to see compassion, sacrifice, forgiveness, understanding, selflessness and unconditional love in action.

From their actions, in faith, I can do all things with and in love. "Little children, let us not love in word or talk but in deed and in truth." (1 John 3:18)

We cannot hide from the truth. A truth we must always choose to speak. A truth to every question asked and every action taken. A truth that does not set us free but gives us freedom.

God, in His divine wisdom, gave us free will. Free will is God's way of saying, "I am here for you. Will you choose Me?"

Our flesh will steer us wrong, steer us in the direction of the enemy every time. The Bible gives us so many ways to live a wonderful, blissful life in Christ. It would be nice if the Bible included a magic potion that makes us do everything right the first time. Oh, wait, it does. Faith.

Faith is all we need to stand firm until God says move. "So I say, walk by the Spirit, and you will not gratify the desires of the flesh." (Galatians 5:16 NIV)

If only life were that simple. Accepting God does not mean you or your life will instantly be changed. Freedom is not free, and free will is not freedom to do whatever you want in life. Free will is an opportunity to show God we accept His love for us. That we willingly choose to walk in His light.

Long before I had the words to describe God's presence, I had music. Songs became the way He whispered to me, the way He wrapped truth within my heart when I was not ready to hear it any other way.

At twelve, when Stephanie Mills sang "Home," I felt God tug me toward Him. At sixteen, George Benson's "The Greatest Love of All" taught me that loving myself mirrored His love for me. Later, music and other songs became the soundtrack of my faith. They carried me when I had no strength of my own.

As I recovered from my stroke, I did not pray to be healed. My prayer was for God to let me dance at my nephew's wedding. I know it sounds crazy. I really did not care if I used a walker or a cane for the rest of my life. All I wanted was the ability to dance, to move to the beat of the music just one more time.

On Sunday, July 10, 2022, I danced, like David danced, all evening at my nephew's wedding. On Monday, July 11, 2022, I was in pain all day. A joy-filled pain. I asked God why dancing was so much more important than walking to me. He started by answering a question I had been asking for years. No, you are not a singer, no, you are not a dancer. Yes, you can sing, yes, you can dance. Singing and dancing are your worship of Me. Your prayers to dance were a plea. To hold onto your connection with Me.

I believe God used music because it touched something in me, slipped past my defenses to reach the heart of me. When sermons felt too sharp or scripture felt too distant, melodies softened me. Music taught me that faith is not only studied. Faith is felt. It touches our souls. It is the hum under our days and the rhythm that lifts and moves us forward.

The one thing we cannot let go of as humans, in our flesh, is that we are not in control. We have to understand that we never had control. We did not have any control from before our conception, and we do not have any control over the outcome of that conception. But we can escape who God birthed us to be.

ACT III
ACCEPTANCE

"I know your deeds. See, I have placed before you an open door that no one can shut. I know that you have little strength, yet you have kept my word and have not denied my name."

(Revelation 3:8 NIV)

Chapter 7

Forgiveness and Family Lessons

"The Jesus Way" - Phil Wickman

Forgiveness is rarely easy. For me, it began with my father. By sixteen, our relationship had completely deteriorated. His presence was inconsistent, and exasperation exploded. I decided I was done. For fourteen years, I lived without allowing him into any space in my life.

God does not let unfinished business stay buried. My mother, who never spoke ill of him, gave my stepmother my phone number. I was furious at both of them. Yet I agreed with my stepmother to reconnect. Every time I saw him, irritation boiled beneath the surface. He was just the same.

Then, after four years of trying and failing to make peace with his presence, I snapped, releasing everything that caused me to distance myself years earlier. All he could say was, "You do not understand. You just do not know."

Something inside me erupted. "Then help me understand." That moment did not erase the past, but it opened a door. Forgiveness did not come overnight. It took prayer, fights with God and time. It started there, with honesty laid bare.

The truth is, my family had been teaching forgiveness long before that moment. My mother encouraged us to see him as more than his failings. My grandparents showed me selflessness and unity. My great aunt lived mercy in action. My great uncle displayed steady grace. I learned that forgiveness is not excusing behavior. It is refusing to operate because of the actions of another that poison who you are. It is keeping your heart free so God can work His healing power.

Teachers and counselors stepped in at the right times, too. Three months before high school graduation, a counselor locked me in her office to keep me from fighting. A fight that would have kept me from graduating. Looking back, she saved more than my diploma. She saved me from derailing my future. Those lessons became the framework of my adolescence and built a spark that would carry me into adulthood.

God placed me within a family and social network to visually see who He is. To learn to appreciate how great the "I Am" truly is. I know I am who I am. It is because of the "I Am" that I am. "Now see that I, even I, Am He, And there is no God besides Me; I kill and I make alive; I wound and I heal; Nor is there any who can deliver from My hand." (Dt 32:39 NKJV)

After accepting Christ, I had an easy time believing in God. Though I did not know Him, I knew His Word. God connected the dots. He gave me the missing pieces to complete the puzzle that is my life.

Knowing God has been the most amazing journey. An adventure I never could have imagined. And my imagination is extensive. God did not create us to leave us. God is with us before conception through eternity. It is truly humbling to understand such a gift and to see how loving God worked in my life even before I acknowledged His existence.

Every fragment of our life, including our time with the enemy, God is with us. He is within our reach, no matter the distance. God chases after us from inception. What we know or do not know of Him is not important. We are important to Him. Just like parents, when a child takes off, He chases us. When we take a moment to be still, we can feel something, hear something that gently turns us back in the right direction. His direction. "The Lord your God in your midst, The Mighty One, will save; He will rejoice over you with gladness, He will quiet you with His love, He will rejoice over you with singing." (Zephaniah 3:17 NKJV)

Chapter 8

Absolute Surrender

"Lord Have Your Way" - Kathy Nichole

The defining moment of my life came thousands of miles from home. Lying in a foreign hospital without any control stripped away the illusion that I could manage my life on my own. This was not just about an affliction. This was an intervention, and God had my attention.

The pride. The delusion of control. The belief that I could steer the ship without Him. All of this brought to mind the last stanza of the poem "Invictus," written during a dark time in the author William Ernest Henley's life. "I am the master of my fate; I am the captain of my soul. Words I used to say a lot. Words I now know are deceptive. God is master, captain, Lord of all."

At forty-eight years, I made the statement, if life is not how I want by age fifty, I will do things my way. A statement I did not even remember making. God did, however, and He knew. So did the enemy.

Before Egypt, I lived with one foot in God's world, one foot in my own. God sent me to Egypt to realize the power of His sovereignty. After returning to Georgia, there was no looking back. My life belonged wholly to Him. He had my instant obedience and absolute surrender.

Absolute surrender is not a single event. It is a conscious choice we have to make daily. It means free-falling without a safety net. Trusting God's hand is under you.

When I look back, I see how He activated His purpose for me in an Egyptian hospital. How for that moment in time, He had been preparing me for His perfect plan. Every song, every joy, every trial, every lesson. He was leading me to that "yes." Egypt was where I agreed in spirit, not just in word and deed. Yes, to His timing. Yes, to God and His way. Yes, to discovering a freedom I have never known. "I pray that out of his glorious riches he may strengthen you with power through his Spirit in your inner being." (Ephesians 3:16 NIV)

Before I got saved, everything I did was simply because I wanted to. God had to compete with all my mess for me to willingly listen, to hear what He had to say. I am visual and analytical. Show me and prove to me. What I found was that God was always willing to indulge all my foolishness, to show me how much I was loved.

Christianity is more than your belief in God. It is having absolute faith in what we cannot see. Getting beyond your fears to knowing beyond any doubt that He is very real. Absolute surrender requires accepting God with a steadfast faith. Absolute surrender, knowing your final answer, your only answer is yes to glorifying the Lord God Almighty.

From the beginning of my journey to my absolute surrender, there were a lot, lot, lot, and many more falls. God never left me alone. He never left me alone when in situations or places I did not belong. He never left me alone when I was callous and calculating. He never left me alone when I turned away.

As Christians, knowing He is always with us, will always forgive us, we justify the conduct we know is unacceptable. "No temptation has overtaken you except such as is common to man; but God is faithful, who will not allow you to be tempted beyond what you are able, but with the temptation will also make the way of escape, that you may be able to bear it." (1 Corinthians 10:13 NKJV)

Even when I did not realize or recognize that He was guiding and directing my steps, many of my falls were caused by my belief that I got it. Then, by letting go of God, thinking, now I can move forward alone. It took years to accept that God and I are glued at the hip. There is nothing I can do, nowhere I can go. He is always right there with me. "Fear not, for I am with you; be not dismayed, for I am your God. I will strengthen you, yes, I will help you, I will uphold you with My righteous right hand." (Isaiah 41:10 NKJV)

As we keep looking up, hands up. God is moving all stumbling blocks in your path. The minute you look down and start to believe with your eyes, you fall over that one block He has yet to remove. We have to rise above ourselves until He determines the time blocks should be moved. Until then, be still, wait and listen to hear the block is gone. "For in this hope we were saved. Now hope that is seen is not hope. For who hopes for what he sees. But if we hope for what we do not see, we wait for it with patience." (Romans 8:24-25 NKJV)

There will be times of constant stumbles and falls, one after another, before we remember to look up. God cannot be other than who He is. He will not make us believe or accept what He freely gives. He will be patiently waiting for when we fall to our knees in absolute surrender, accepting that we cannot do anything alone, in our own strength.

When you stand in absolute surrender, when you stand upon His firm foundation, our steady rock, have faith in why you believe. Truly know, fully believe who God is to you, for you, in you. "Do you not know that you are God's temple and that God's Spirit dwells in you?" (1 Corinthians 3:16 NIV)

Chapter 9

A Legacy of Service and Discipleship

"God Did It" by Micah Tyler

When I look back over my life, I can clearly see how, from the beginning, God directed my path, leading me to where I am now. I see how much has been shaped not only by what I received but by what I am called to give. Service has always been the thread that tied my story together, even before I had a language for it. The blueprint for how I live today.

From my grandparents, I inherited compassion and resilience. My grandfather's unwavering truth, my grandmother's caring, my great aunt's concern, my great uncle's kindness, and my mother's loyalty. Love is not just something you say. Love is something you do.

In Miami and later in Atlanta, that legacy took form. I volunteered with nonprofits, chaired boards, and built a business that supported organizations serving others. I was drawn to teens and seniors, to those on either end of the spectrum, lost in the shuffle of the world. Those who sometimes need a reminder that they are seen and heard.

None of it was part of a master plan. It simply felt right to answer a pull inside. I can see that service was never only about helping others. Service is my calling, God's way of shaping me into a Disciple of Christ.

Christianity is more than belief; it is action. It is walking as Jesus walked and carrying His love into places where people may not be ready to hear His Word but can feel His presence through us. We may not know where that walk will take us, but we will definitely spend a lot of time walking in circles if we do not walk in surrender and obedience.

We confuse fire and brimstone as a representation of Christ. It took a while for me to want any part of being a Christian. Finally accepting Christ, the Old Testament, helped me understand God, not Christ or Christianity. "Each of you should use whatever gift you have received to serve others, as faithful stewards of God's grace in its various forms." (1 Peter 4:10 NIV)

As I walked my Christian journey, the Old and New Testaments were two separate books, with no straightforward relevance between them. I loved the Old Testament, the no-holds barred, upfront, in-your-face actions of God. It all made perfect sense to me. The New Testament was such a hodgepodge of jumbled, perplexing words that left me baffled. The New Testament, so different from the Old Testament, seemed to have no direct relationship. The Old Testament equaled the Wild Wild West, God shoots from the hip, while the New Testament was more like welcome to my neighborhood, with Jesus as Mr. Rogers, won't you be my neighbor.

In preparation to write *Hear The Father, Rise Beyond Self*, the two worlds came together. I finally understood the New Testament in relation to the Old Testament. The Old Testament: why we believe in God, the New Testament: how we believe in Jesus. The world usually puts the emphasis on the why. God will supply my needs. Most Christians focus on the distorted version, believing God will give them everything they want, completely missing that God will supply all their needs to do the work of Christ. "And God is able to bless you abundantly, so that in all things at all times, having all that you need, you will abound in every good work." (2 Corinthians 9:8 NIV)

We need to place equal weight on the how, doing the work of Christ. Jesus saved us. He died on the cross for our sins. Doing the work we are called to do keeps us from nailing Jesus to the cross again and again and again. "For the message of the cross is foolishness to those who are perishing, but to us who are being saved it is the power of God." (1 Corinthians 1:18 NIV)

I believe Christians think their only part in salvation is bringing others to Christ. We have to realize that the continuousness of salvation is evolving into a Disciple of Christ. Jesus died on the Cross for our sins so that we can walk in freedom on earth until our time in eternity with God. Walking is an action. We have to move to help believers live as Christ. "For we are His workmanship, created in Christ Jesus for good works, which God prepared beforehand that we should walk in them." (Ephesians 2:10 NKJV)

Growing up, I heard the "Jana" stories, the theme, the stubborn consistency. Stubbornness opened the door for the enemy, and consistency gave me the strength to finally walk out that door.

Leaving New York was more than a geographical move. It was the beginning of my spiritual journey. Learning life is not all about me, about choices rippling outward. My life affects all those I touch. Georgia was never my choice as a final destination. So, never could I have imagined that Georgia was where I would find my true self. All of me coming together. The self, connected to the God within me. "But the seed on good soil stands for those with a noble and good heart, who hear the word, retain it, and by persevering produce a crop." (Luke 8:15)

Pieces and parts of me got scrambled, trying to break free of invisible chains. That is, until remembering the teachings from my childhood. All of me merged, bringing together who I was, who I can be, who I will be, and who I am.

I spend a lot of time trying to stretch my wings. To be free. Then the light bulb came on, and the light came through. Freedom is not breaking away. Freedom is being permanently shackled to the life God prepared from the beginning. There were no invisible chains, only the loving arms of God wrapped around me. "In truthful speech and in the power of God; with weapons of righteousness in the right hand and in the left;" (2 Corinthians 6:7 NIV)

ACT IV
ACKNOWLEDGE

"Yet to all who did receive him, to those who believed in his name,
he gave the right to become children of God."

(John 1:12 NIV)

Chapter 10

The Path Jesus Laid

"Ain't Nobody Like Jesus" - Cody Carnes

We can only know what we do not know once we know it. Christians have to do more than tell others about Christ. Christians have to help those who come to Christ understand and know the reason for Christ. For me, I would have spent more time with God and gotten baptized once if someone, anyone, had helped me understand I have to know Christ, not just believe in God.

We do not have to be pastors or theologians to guide others to have a personal relationship with God. And in that personal relationship, we will grasp the fullness of Christ.

Family and friends all take part in teaching a child to grow into a responsible adult. Christians have that same responsibility to teach how to grow into Disciples of Christ. "For I have given you an example, that you should do as I have done to you. Most assuredly, I say to you, a servant is not greater than his master; nor is he who is sent greater than he who sent him." (John 13:15-16 NKJV)¶

Five years after accepting Christ, someone in a Bible Study class asked me how much time I spent alone with God in His Word. She was surprised when I said none, then shocked when I said I was not going into a closet to talk to anyone. I read God's Word and spent time talking to Him. I just did not believe I needed to be doing it inside a closet. She then explained that "in the closet" meant your quiet place or time to be alone with God. That would have been nice to know five years earlier. I guess it was a good thing I was already doing it. "And the things that you have heard from me among many witnesses, commit these to faithful men who will be able to teach others also." (2 Timothy 2:2 NKJV)

Not long after that, in another Bible Study class on baptism, I learned I did not understand the covenant and commitment I was making to God when I was baptized. My first baptism was two years after accepting Christ. It was simply to keep Christians from pestering me for not being baptized. Baptism was presented as the next step to be "truly saved." Again, no one really explained what it meant to be baptized.

I decided to get baptized the second time, being fully conscious of what I was doing, of why and what it meant. My second baptism was a true spiritual experience at a lake in the mountains. Most amazing, Jesus was right there in the water with me. Jesus held His hand to my chest, asking if I was ready for my life to fully belong to God. Telling me, "Know that once you come up out of the water, you will never be the same."

I said, "Yes, Jesus, let me up to begin my new life in Christ."

"And this water symbolizes baptism that now saves you also—not the removal of dirt from the body but the pledge of a clear conscience toward God. It saves you by the resurrection of Jesus Christ." (1 Peter 3:21 NIV)

Now, the best advice I received after salvation: God is real. Treat Him the same as family and friends. That is how I started to live my relationship with God after my baptism in the lake. How I will continue to live for the rest of my life. I talk to God, spend time with God, and I fuss and fight with God. I roll my eyes at God, stomping my feet as I follow the path, He called me to walk. My personal relationship with God is just as tangible as with family and friends. We have to know our relationship with God is worthy and worth what we put into our relationship with family and friends. Family is family, making friends is easy. Building a relationship with either that stands the test of time takes a whole lot of work.

As Christians, I believe our duty is to teach and show others how we become Disciples of Christ. "Therefore, go and make disciples of all nations, baptizing them in the name of the Father and of the Son and of the Holy Spirit." (Matthew 28:19)

Chapter 11

Live Heaven on Earth

"Millions" - The Winans

I think the hardest thing for a Christian to believe or understand is that Heaven is our home. Earth, this world is only our temporary residence, where we get to do the work of Jesus while we are able to worship God in spirit and in truth, as we wait for the day, we are with Him in glory. "For now, we see only a reflection as in a mirror; then we shall see face to face. Now I know in part; then I shall know fully, even as I am fully known. (1 Corinthians 13:12 NIV)

Heaven was the make-or-break decision for me as to whether or not I would continue moving forward with God or go my own way. If Heaven were real, then Hell had to be equally as real. If there is a place we want to go, then there has to be a place we do not want to go.

I do not know if my mother was saved when she died, which would mean no Heaven for her. I spent a lot of time struggling with God on this, trying to understand. God spoke to me with His word. "For he says, 'In the time of my favor I heard you, and in the day of salvation I helped you. I tell you, now is the time of God's favor, now is the day of salvation." (2 Corinthians 6:2 NIV)

Next, I saw the movie *Five People We Meet in Heaven*. The movie made Heaven or the possibility of Heaven more than a mystical place. More than where lives are wonderful in Lala Land. The movie allowed me to get a perspective on the concept of Heaven and Hell. An awareness, I know I would not have gotten, trying to understand on my own. God gives us the opportunity for Heaven until our last breath. *Five People We Meet in Heaven* helped me interpret what hope feels like, looks like. How scary it is to be a Christian.

Then God spoke again, about the thief on the cross. What maybe she did or thought with her last breath. I am a realist. Bottom line, realistically, I did not, do not know if my mother accepted Christ. What I do know is my faith. That continual leap we have to take for our relationship with God to grow. "Therefore, my heart rejoiced, and my tongue was glad; Moreover, my flesh also will rest in hope." (Acts 2:26 NKJV)

We get so focused on where we are now that we do not think a lot about where we are going. We are grounded in this world, feet firmly planted in the earth. That focus started to change for me during my years of back-to-back health issues. It caused me to rethink everything I knew or thought I knew after my stroke.

As I mentioned earlier, God got my attention in a place I never intended to visit. I always wanted to go to Morocco, and my family wanted to go to Egypt, so we combined the two trips. We went to Morocco first. I had a great time. Morocco is a beautiful country, as wonderful as I expected. As for Egypt, I remember arriving and visiting the Pyramids. Next, I recall waking up in a hospital, being told I had a stroke. I love cruising, and the only part of Egypt I was excited about was cruising the Nile. I am told I went on that cruise. I do not remember getting on or off the ship.

After waking up the first time and finally somewhat grasping what had happened, there was never a time I thought that I was going to die. God and I had numerous conversations about my death staged as an act of quietly going to sleep. By waking up, I knew I would eventually recover. After leaving the hospital and preparing to fly home, then waking up again in the hospital, all I could do was cry. What scared me about dealing with a disability in a foreign country was accepting the realization that I had absolutely no control over anything. "Many are the plans in a person's heart, but it is the Lord's purpose that prevails." (Psalms 19:21)

You have a lot of time to think and reflect, in a foreign hospital, watching the same three movies all day on the one English-speaking channel. The first time in the hospital, I was not listening to anyone. I just kept saying, "I want to go home." The second time, I knew this was God's way of getting my attention. I rarely make promises and only to God. I promised God if He got me out of Egypt, back to Atlanta, I would do it His way for the rest of my life.

After that, I felt at peace. I still did not know what would happen, but I was at peace. Even though I stayed in the Egyptian hospital for almost four weeks, I knew with everything in me, I was going home. Making that promise was exactly what God was waiting to hear from me. God sent me to a place I never wanted to go, for me to give Him complete reign over my life.

We are all created for the glory of God. As His own unique design, here on Earth is where we fulfill His purpose. I learned a permanent, never-to-be-forgotten lesson. God literally brought me out of Egypt with riches. And during my three years of recovery, God got "the Egypt" out of me. "He brought out Israel, laden with silver and gold, and from among their tribes no one faltered." (Psalm 105:37)

My willingness to surrender finally opened my heart to hear God's final answer to me, always questioning everything, "for your growth and my glory."

I went to New York thinking it was to see the Fiftieth Anniversary of *The Wiz* on Broadway. When I found myself crying outside a gift shop on the corner of Times Square and Broadway, the truth hit me hard. God sent me to New York to say goodbye.

I held on to being a New Yorker so tightly, not wanting to lose what I thought was my home, my stability, what meant family to me. I will always remember the dizzying feeling as I looked up, not seeing the

New York I knew, realizing it was no longer my home. It was just another place I have lived here on Earth.

God gives us the opportunity to experience Heaven on Earth. Something we do not always appreciate. Earth is the place we live, where we get to know God and do the work of Christ. Where others get to see His glory through us. Only God knows when it is time for us to say goodbye, when the battle is over. When our time in the home we cling to on Earth is finished. When we can rest with Him in our eternal home in Heaven. "For our citizenship is in Heaven, from which we also eagerly wait for the Savior, the Lord Jesus Christ." (Philippians 3:20 NKJV)

Chapter 12

Free to Know Freedom

"Testimony" - Terrian

The world has gone through so much of what "has never been." 2024 was my year of rest, isolation and private time with God. My time to hear where I am, and how I got here. To learn how I move forward, to understand my never is now.

I developed allergies that caused a severe rash and stopped up my ears, somewhat like the feeling of waiting for your ears to pop after a plane landing. Then one morning, my ears were clear. I woke up to hear the two-sided coin. Years ago, I started picking pennies off the ground, declaring each time I trust you, Lord. Over time, every penny was not just a penny. They were my moments to stop. To give thanks to God. Hear His direction. Confirmation that I was on the right path.

We see coins all the time. However, we probably do not spend all that much time examining the coins. Coins have two sides, produced in a facility that mints coins. Minting stamps both sides at the same time. Sometimes mishaps occur, only fully minting one side. Astoundingly, a one-sided minted coin has more worth than the actual penny value. That coin is rare, its value determined by what the collector will pay. The value increases if minting creates a double imperfection.

Now, imagine the enemy as a coin, always waiting on either side to confuse our worth. Trying to make us believe there is value in the trouble he fabricates in our lives. As Christians, we have to weigh our value by *whose* we are. We have to know we are listening to God. Hearing what God is saying versus the value we place on what we hope to hear.

God called to me three or four times before I finally heard His call. He is always waiting on the sidelines for us. While He is waiting, with our backs to Him, He is guiding and directing our steps. Helping us to remember the value He placed on us. "For what profit is it to a man if he gains the whole world, and loses his own soul? Or what will a man give in exchange for his soul?" (Matthew 16:26 NKJV)

God sent me home with my mother at two months old to keep me near to Him with my grandfather. God sent me home at eight years old to keep me near to Him with a clear mind to learn. God sent me home at twelve years old to keep me near to Him with a heart for music. God lost me at sixteen years old when I placed the enemy's value of me over God's. Yet, all that He already placed in me did not fade away. It just got lost in the confusion of the enemy. "But My people would not heed My voice, And Israel would have none of Me. So, I gave them over to their own stubborn heart, to walk in their own counsels." (Psalm 81:11-12 NKJV)

God and I have been connected my entire life. Even while I was enthralled in the enemy's camp, God stayed connected to me, especially through my grandfather and music. This connection made it easier for me to reconnect to Him when I got saved. My ears stopped up because I was listening to the enemy, not hearing God. By not hearing, I moved in my own strength, making life happen by my interpretation. My focus was distracted, like on a treadmill moving but going nowhere. I did not completely understand the value of what I was missing. I did not follow the path God wanted me to travel.

God knows us better than anyone, more than we know ourselves. God is with us everywhere, always covering and protecting us. However, God gave us free will, meaning He will let us go our way, always waiting for when we are listening to hear His call.

I am a "Trekkie," a *Star Trek* fan. From the second *Star Trek* series, *The Next Generation*, a theme developed, being integrated throughout all the subsequent series: The Borg, a cybernetic species. Their objective is to alter the DNA of other species to control their minds. The Borg roam the galaxy to assimilate other sentient beings into one interconnected whole called a "Collective." The Borg has the capacity to quickly adapt their thoughts and reactions to other species, lasting for centuries, with the ability to instantly acquire strategic knowledge from their perceived enemies. The "Collective" existed as a single unit, operating in unison with one unified thought.

God is calling us, His children, to join His collective. To be of one mind, one heart, moving in harmony for His glory. The difference: joining God's collective is a choice. We get to decide for ourselves whether to connect to Him. God is not going to assimilate us. He wants us to freely choose Him, to want to change and grow in the image of Christ. "Fulfill my joy by being like-minded, having the same love, being of one accord, of one mind." (Philippians 2:2 NKJV)

As we continue to move forward, we have to know God intimately. As we grow into Disciples of Christ, we have to be on the same frequency with His mind and heart. We have to quickly restructure how we think about what He knows. "For the word of God *is* living and powerful, and sharper than any two-edged sword, piercing even to the division of soul and spirit, and of joints and marrow, and is a discerner of the thoughts and intents of the heart. (Hebrews 4:12 NKJV)

After a year of listening, 2025 was my year of connection, bringing all elements into a fuller understanding, creating a new tapestry of my life.

In the Prologue, I explained how I started writing *Hear The Father, Rise Beyond Self*. The day after, I spoke with a friend about what was said in the Sunday program, asking and/or stating why people do not understand, you always have to be your authentic self. While she agreed about always being your authentic self, what she said next stunned me. My friend thought I was combative about being authentically me. She felt I argued just to get a reaction.

Later, I really thought about what she said. Although I completely disagreed, this was not the first time someone said I was combative or confrontational. It did make me wonder: Is this a way of saying I am too passionate and expressive? Or is this an excuse to deflect their fear of how others will react to their authentic self? Then, I asked myself, am I fighting myself, not allowing someone to change who I am? Finally, I thought, either way, I only know how to be me. If who I am makes me "too" whatever, so be it.

The one thing I've learned in all my years before and after becoming a Christian is that standing strong for what you believe and know to be the truth takes courage. "For no other foundation can anyone lay than that which is laid, which is Jesus Christ." (1 Corinthians 3:11 NKJV)

Courage comes from the Old French "corage" with heart. In French, courage refers to the strength of mind in regard to danger. We are in battle with our flesh every day. Discipleship requires courage. As Christians, we must find the strength to face the danger we bring upon ourselves when we choose to follow Christ. When we hide from the truth that we are called to be Disciples of Christ, we place ourselves at war with ourselves—with our own hearts. The truth, our lives are led with God and led by God. "Have I not commanded you, be strong and of good courage; do not be afraid, nor be dismayed, for the Lord your God *is* with you wherever you go." (Joshua 1:9 NKJV)

I was slapped in the face once in my life by a dental nurse. As I was trying to wake up and process the sensation of being slapped, I heard my friend screaming and the nurse yelling. I had oral surgery with instructions to my friend, let me sleep and leave when I wake up. The slap was because I never woke up. The nurse failed to include in her instructions to wake me after a certain period of time. This scenario or situation is how we stay trapped by the enemy, afraid and scared of what comes next.

God does not give us incomplete instructions; he just does not give us all our instructions at one time. When we think we received complete instructions from God, we move full steam ahead. Then, when the situation does not go as we thought, we accept the misinformation the enemy feeds to fill in the blanks. "Count it all joy, my brothers, when you meet trials of various kinds, for you know that the testing of your faith produces steadfastness. And let steadfastness have its full effect, that you may be perfect and complete, lacking in nothing." (James 1:2-4 NKJV)

I asked God in the beginning stages of my salvation to let me see what was coming. He very clearly said no, that if I knew all ahead of time, my focus would be on getting to the end. I think that is true for many of us. God does not want us to just get through. He wants us to go through. When we go through, we grow. After twenty-five years of periodic asking, I finally got the message, "You do not have to know to go."

We have to know God is fully aware of everything that happens in our lives, and in every aspect of the world around us. He already knows it will happen. We will make free will choices that He does not want for us. Freedom costs. Free will is a tool for us to accept and reiterate to ourselves that we freely choose Him every day.

God must always be our light, any time of day or night, to guide us where we need to go. To begin seeing His light, we have to go to His Word and know His Word. "Your word *is* a lamp to my feet and a light to my path." (Psalm 119:105 NKJV)

The Bible gives everything and anything we need to be a Christian and live as a Disciple of Christ. The first time I realized that was when He showed me in His word on how to buy clothes. I was wasting my money on fabric that did not last, that was not meant to be knit together. I am literal. God's word is not. It speaks truth to facts we have yet to recognize exactly as written. The Bible gives us full instructions God does not allow us to completely see all at once.

The intent of God's word is timeless. As people of the twenty-first century, we have to hear what He says, take what He has written, and understand for that moment in time. We have to move without changing or adding what we want to His word. We do not have Moses, or Joshua, or any of the disciples. However, we do have and will always have God's word. His unwavering guidance directs us and brings us home. We have to be intentional in living out His word. To live our lives applying His counsel to the time we are living in now.

God knew time would not stand still. God already knows all. Do not let the enemy take you off course, down a path, thinking God's word is not relevant centuries later. "All Scripture *is* given by inspiration of God, and *is* profitable for doctrine, for reproof, for correction, for instruction in righteousness, that the man of God may be complete, thoroughly equipped for every good work." (2 Timothy 3:16-17 NKJV)

Go to God every day; let Jesus' sacrifice on the cross not be in vain. Going through the last ten years of my life, 2015 through 2025, was to me, my time of the Israelites roaming in the desert, Job losing everything and Paul's conversion on the road to Damascus. Would I have wanted any of it? No. Did I need to go through all of it? Yes. Why? For who I am, the only way I would embrace my calling, live my purpose and give all glory to God. For you, it will be different. How different is for you to decide. But understand, once you know the truth, you are responsible to live that truth.

God prepared us and covers us. We grow and stretch in Him as we fulfill our purpose on this Earth. I know I am because of the "All Mighty I Am." Although it has been said for and against, the idea that the Bible tells us in 365 ways not to fear or be afraid. There is no debate. We can go to His word 365 days a year, where we find the truth, the strength, and the will to continue onward.

"And David said to his son Solomon, 'Be strong and of good courage, and do it; do not fear nor be dismayed, for the Lord God—my God—

will be with you. He will not leave you nor forsake you, until you have finished all the work for the service of the house of the Lord.'"
(1 Chronicles 28:20 NKJV)

EPILOGUE

"I Believe You" - Megan Wood

Rise Above Self
"Still I Rise" - Yolanda Adams

The phrase "when they go low, we go high" used to really bother me. I could not understand why you were even that low. Then I read an explanation that made it make sense to me. To "go high" is to respond with a heart guided by wisdom rather than emotion—doing the inner work to rise above with patience and understanding and leading with compassion and grace that opens the way for growth and healing in others. I now see its meaning as a state of mind— a mindset shift that allows us to grow in our purpose.

Another phrase that seems senseless to me is, "What would Jesus do?" As Christians, we know what Jesus would do; we know what Jesus did. The question is, what are you doing? Maybe, again, I am being too literal. As flesh and blood, we will never be able to do what Jesus did. We can have the mind of Christ. We can ask ourselves, am I following the path of Jesus? Am I doing the work God has called me to do in the name of Jesus? Will I hear, well done, good and faithful servant? "Whoever serves me must follow me; and where I am, my servant also will be. My Father will honor the one who serves me." (John 12:26)

As Disciples of Christ, we have to renew our minds, change our mindset on what it is to be a servant, to serve, and to be of service. I have worked in the service industry or in customer service, serving people since I was sixteen years old, and I can say it is by the grace of God that I survived.

What I grew to learn is that all people want is someone who cares about their concerns. Someone who will take the time to listen. Someone to put them first. I survived because I learned to be a servant leader. Jesus was a servant leader. Being a servant first means caring for those around you, then teaching how to become a leader. Committed leaders teach others how to be of service. We have to change our worldly thinking that service and serving are demeaning. As disciples, we are serving God as servants of Christ. "Do not conform to the pattern of this world but be transformed by the renewing of your mind. Then you will be able to test and approve what God's will is—his good, pleasing and perfect will." (Romans 12:2)

You are a Christian wherever you are. Ask God when in that space, "Why am I here? What are you calling me to do?" If you are being obedient, God places you where you are supposed to be, to do the work of Christ. Discipleship cannot just fit into your schedule or be a check mark off your daily to-do list. Disciples are God's messengers. We have to spend time with and interact with people who we may think are not worth our time.

The Gospels Matthew, Mark and Luke each mention a phrase I would use as an excuse to justify walking away: "shaking the dust from your feet or sandals." Disciples cannot just arbitrarily walk away. God calls us to the place where He needs His message to be heard. A message He sent specifically for you to convey in word or through service. If the message is not being heard, we do not walk away; we walk on. We do not look back to see what others are doing. We do not stop to compare whose work is better. We stay focused, continue the journey until God says it is finished.

Discipleship is not convenient. We hinder ourselves from doing the work of Christ for a list of reasons. The most pervasive, I believe, is fear. Fear we are not good enough, smart enough, or anything we can think of enough. How you are called, why you are called, and where you are called only matter to God. Focus on His call for you to serve. As you start to move, He will walk with you through the fear.

God used the arts for me as the avenue to help me know who He is and how to become a Disciple of Christ. Music, songs, dance, movies, television, theater, etc. I look in all of them to find God's message.

Watching Westerns is how He showed me to stop comparing myself to some invisible standard of someone else. There is always a fast gunfighter. What made them fast was not just their skill with a gun. It was knowing they could die at any moment. Not that they wanted to die, it was just the reality of the choice they made. No matter how fast they were or thought they were, gunfighters knew there would always be someone coming to take their place as top gun. Someone who may be faster out of the holster. Yet, just to prove they were the best, the fastest, they were willing to stand up against anyone who threatened their perceived ability. Though I do love watching Westerns for the gunfights, that mentality never made sense to me.

Other genres that hold my attention are action, crime, drama, mystery and thrillers. I watch the different genres for various reasons. I watch them all to see if I can determine what they will do. I try to figure out, for good or bad, how far they will go to win. I may be watching a movie; however, that is how we live our lives, by putting all our efforts into winning, grabbing the prize, and being the best.

I am very competitive and will give my all to win. However, I am good with who I am, if I lose. My grandfather told me, always be happy when you know you did your best. Never forget, no matter how good you are, someone is going to lose, and that someone could be you.

God's lesson in what I watch: There will always be someone who thinks they are better than you. They will come from all directions, behind you, next to you, right in front of you. You need to think, is this the stand you really want to take? The hill you want to die on? Ask yourself, why do I need to prove myself? Who am I trying to convince, the crowd or myself?

God wants all our efforts and energy to go into knowing Him, following Jesus, rather than putting our efforts and energy into trying to come out on top. "Am I now trying to win the approval of human beings, or of God? Or am I trying to please people? If I were still trying to please people, I would not be a servant of Christ." (Galatians 1:10 NIV).

Even if you win every time, there will always be someone greater who you will never defeat. Trust me, I tried. As you focus on those around you, make sure you also focus on the One above you. God wants you to remember that you have to prove yourself to no one. You have already been certified, approved, and justified—walk in the truth of who you are. To Him who called you and created you for His purpose. "I am the Alpha and the Omega," says the Lord God, "who is, and who was, and who is to come, the Almighty." (Revelation 1:8 NIV)

As I think about my life, everything I do involves first organizing things in my mind. I love figuring out how all the pieces fit together into one complete picture. As we journey from Christian to Disciple of Christ, we continually learn to fit the facets of our lives into God's divine design.

I have been able to study, learn and discern the Word of God to live in the will of God as He intended for me. Only He knows what we need to live the life destined especially for each of us. A life that will glorify Him.

As we stay the course, we develop our personal relationship with Him. We grow into a Disciple of Christ. "Jesus answered, "I am the way and the truth and the life. No one comes to the Father except through me." (John 14:6 NIV)

Our life is God's own individual, unique creation for us. *Hear The Father, Rise Beyond Self,* is my journey, my personal relationship with God. How I strive to walk in His strength every day, knowing I never walk alone. To hear His truth, to be who He designed me to be. To always remember "God Is Not Against Me." – Elevation Worship.

My prayer for you is to believe in you and trust in Him. Ask God to show you whose you are. That you hear Him calling you "Against All

Odds" – Phil Collins, as you take that leap of faith, to rise above self and let your spirit soar in freedom as you Rise Beyond Self.

I KNOW WHY

What a feeling, my thoughts alive in you
I give everything, surrender all to you
Your Word deep within, my heart beats for you
You are my reason why

What a feeling you bring to my soul
United together, spirit to spirit
You will always be a part of me
You are my reason why

What a feeling to have you in my life
The road we travel will never end
Our destiny together, a dream come true
You are my reason why

What a feeling to know your love
Joined forever, needing no other
Your perfect plan, my perfect reality
You are my reason why

Jana L. Johnson
December 3, 2023

"I said, "Oh, that I had the wings of a dove!
I would fly away and be at rest."
(Psalm 55:6 NIV)